A souvenir guide

Rainham Hall

London

Jenny Collett

Contents

Our Big House

Robust and dignified, Rainham Hall was built to last.

The Hall stands proudly at the centre of Rainham village, in the London Borough of Havering. By aristocratic standards, the Hall is a modest house, but when it was built for Captain John Harle in 1729 it must have been a building of some significance, in both size and architecture, just as it still is today.

The Hall is a rare survivor and a wonderful example of early 18th-century architecture. It was designed as a home, not for the super-rich, but for the 'middling sort' of successful maritime merchant. It was built to be lived in and used.

After being requisitioned in the Second World War, the Hall's survival was uncertain. Eventually the National Trust took it over but it was let out to tenants with limited public access. Now fully reopened to the public, and the fabric of the building conserved for future generations to enjoy, it is hoped Rainham Hall will be a focal point in a vibrant and diverse local community.

Rainham before the Hall

In the early 18th century, Rainham was a small village in the rural Thameside landscape. Cattle and sheep were fattened on the marshes to the south for the London market. Fields to the north were sown with crops. The little River Ingrebourne ran down to the Thames. Its tidal section, below the Red Bridge, was called Rainham Creek. Sailing barges came up as far as they could, bringing supplies for the farmers and taking their agricultural produce back to London. From a wharf and alehouse at the mouth of the creek, there were ferries to London and across the river to the Kent shore.

The Thames was a super-highway for shipping, connecting London with the rest of the world. At the time, roads were muddy, rutted and sometimes plagued by highwaymen; consequently water transport was often a better bet. East India merchant ships carrying tea, spices and silk; sugar ships from the Caribbean; ships from Scandinavia, Europe and the American colonies; fishing fleets and whalers; and numerous coastal vessels, all passed Rainham.

Today there is little left of the Rainham Captain John Harle knew – only the church, the Vicarage, Redberry House (both opposite the church) and, of course, Rainham Hall. He would also remember the names of the alehouses, the Phoenix, the Angel and the Bell; even though the buildings are different, they are on their original sites.

Right Rainham has been home to a number of very different inhabitants since it was first built in 1729

Opposite, below right This map from 1806 shows Rainham's situation in Essex

Piecing together the past

Up to now, the story of Rainham Hall was based on a 1920s *Country Life* magazine article, some of which was unproven. As part of the conservation project, a team of volunteers set out to rediscover the history of the Hall and those who lived here.

Rainham Hall was not occupied by generations of one family so there are no piles of papers and family heirlooms hidden in the attic or lurking in cupboards (though that's not to say interesting objects – such as coins, children's toys and old bus tickets – haven't been discovered in the building). Its owners were not aristocratic or famous, so the remaining evidence of their lives is buried in dusty documents scattered across national and county archives. Piecing together these fragments into a coherent story has been a fascinating experience.

We've also discovered more about Rainham's many residents, including a cycling-enthusiast vicar, nursery children, a *Vogue* photographer, musicians and art collectors. Over the coming years, a changing programme of events and displays, each focusing on a resident, will bring the Hall alive again – to be inhabited and used, this time by you, our visitors.

So, who's living at Rainham Hall today? Knock on the door, come inside and explore.

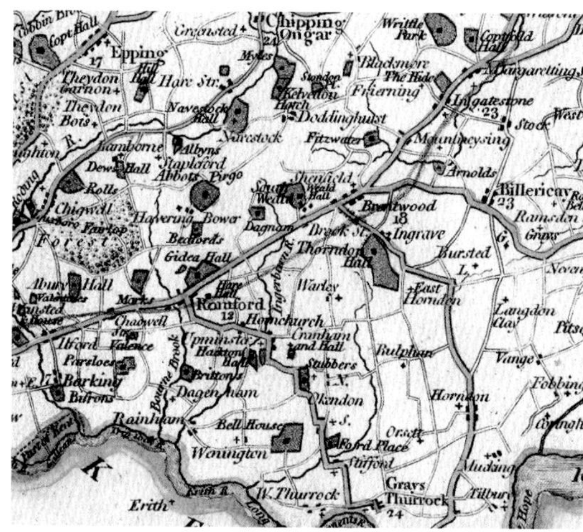

John Harle

Rainham Hall was the vision of a northern maritime man.

The son of a South Shields mariner, John Harle (1688–1742) was one of six brothers, one elder (George) and four younger (Richard, James, Joshua and William). Their father, also John, died in 1704; he had owned a leasehold farm in the area where many such farmers supplemented their income with craft production or maritime activities.

The South Shields area was particularly famous for shipping coal to London, which depended on the fuel. It's thought that by 1700 about 500 colliers – John's father among them – were carrying nearly a million tons of coal to the capital every year.

We know nothing of John Harle's early life, but, with his father often away at sea, he probably helped with farming activities and at relatives' salt pans. However, he certainly had a good level of education because, as an adult, he could read, write and do accounts. He would have grown up around boats and ships, perhaps going to sea from the age of eight on ships his father part-owned.

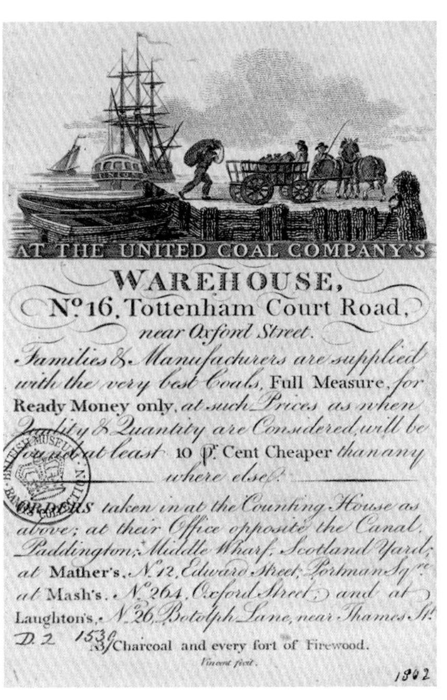

The coal trade

The family ships passed down through the brothers from George to John and, by 1714, to their youngest brother William. The East Coast coal fleet was known as the 'nursery of the Navy' because it produced tough, experienced sailors. When Britain was at war, colliers' crews were often taken by Navy press gangs. John Harle, along with his father and brother George, were granted protection documents against impressment so they could continue to supply London with coal and shipbuilding materials.

Some ships were devoted to the coal run, but the Harles began to concentrate on the Baltic trade and, later, the Mediterranean. By the 1720s, John Harle, who commanded the ship *Mary,* and his brothers Richard, captain of the *Harle*, and William, of the *Mediterranean*, were taking cargoes from Lisbon, Leghorn, Messina, Venice, Zante, as well as Amsterdam and Hamburg, to Sweden and Russia. They carried wheat, salt, fish, wine, dried fruit, Russian leather, wax and even caviar.

Life on land

In 1704, George inherited the farm in South Shields and gradually stopped going to sea. Sometime after 1704 the other Harle brothers settled in London, in the crowded maritime community of St Katherine's and Wapping where they had business and family connections. In 1719, John Harle married Mary Tibbington, a widow (perhaps explaining the name of his ship).

Two of John's brothers, James and Joshua, chose land-based careers and married. His other brothers, Richard and William, continued to work at sea. Between voyages they lodged with John and Mary. Although they were away for two years or more at a time, they only stayed in port a few months before setting sail again.

After his marriage, John seldom went to sea. Eventually, he handed command of the *Mary* to a young cousin, Ralph Harle. John concentrated on the land-based side of the business, frequenting the Royal Exchange and City coffee houses where shipping information could be gathered and trading deals sealed.

John Harle came to Rainham in 1728. We think he acquired the land there from Thomas Williford (see page 6), a member of John's local parish council, St Botolph Aldgate, where John was an officer. He likely met Williford unloading colliers on the Thames. John resigned from St Botolph Aldgate in May 1728 and in December that year was elected to Rainham's parish council.

Far left *Brighton Beach, with Colliers*, 1824, John Constable. Oil on paper. The image depicts coal ships like the ones the Harles may have commanded

Left *The Coffee-house Politicians*, 1722, anonymous artist. This is the sort of place Harle may have done business

Top A trade card for the United Coal Company (1818, unknown artist). East Coast ships brought coal down to London for merchants like these

Building Rainham Hall

From 1718 to 1722, the land on which Rainham Hall would be built a few years later, and a wharf on Rainham Creek, were part of a legal dispute. The owner, William Arnold, and his rogue son-in-law, Cornelius Denne, were involved in a Virginian tobacco deal that went seriously wrong.

Arnold transferred the land to Thomas Williford, allegedly fraudulently, so his creditors couldn't take it. We don't know the outcome of the legal case, but perhaps John Harle bought the land from Williford, as Williford sank into debt.

Documents say there was a farmhouse with barns, orchard and fishpond already on the land, as well as buildings at the wharf. John must have demolished the old house when he built the Hall.

Arnold and then Williford supplied the area with goods, especially coal, from the wharf on the creek. John took over this business and expanded it to include building materials and agricultural products and, probably, a passenger service between London and Rainham.

Inside the Hall

We don't know who designed and built the Rainham Hall we see today, nor how much it cost. Only a lead rainwater hopper tells us it was built in 1729.

Harle's Hall looks more like a London merchant's town house than a country villa. The large entrance hall, used for public-facing events, was – intentionally – a little old-fashioned even when new – though it, and its niche, was an 18th-century status symbol. The smaller parlours to the side of the Hall were for family and close friends.

Left The entrance hall would have been used for public-facing events

Above The impressive staircase, carved from Caribbean mahogany

Below right The iron gates feature John and Mary's entwined initials

Fashion-forward?

The grand staircase is unusual in that the handrail and balustrade are carved from Caribbean mahogany. Oak would have been more usual at this time; mahogany was not then a fashionable and expensive furniture wood, but was used to stabilise cargoes in homebound ships. Did John Harle merely pick up a bargain on a London wharf or was he pre-empting a trend?

Other special original features you can see today include the railings at the front of the building, much of the room panelling, the carvings above the door frames, and the ornate central Porch complete with columns.

Tragedy and a ray of light

Did people in the 18th century accept the inevitability of death more than we do today? John Harle was orphaned by age 16 and three of his brothers had passed away by 1737, as had one of their wives and several of their babies. In 1737, his cousin Ralph also lost his life, and his ship, when attacked by the Spanish in the Caribbean.

Sometime in 1739, Mary died childless. John remarried quite soon afterwards, to Sarah Gregory, a widow who lived in Rainham. It must have been a joyous day when Sarah gave birth to their only child, also John, in 1740.

The end of the Harle era

Although John stated he was 'of sound health' when writing his will in February 1742, he died just ten months later. He is buried inside Rainham Church.

Left with a small son to care for, Sarah advertised Rainham Hall and wharf to let in 1743. It seems she may have rented out the wharf but continued to live in the Hall. Her god-daughter, Sarah Green, and widowed sister, Jane Vincent, joined her there.

Tragedy struck again in 1749 when Sarah Harle died, leaving the orphaned John junior in her sister Jane's care. Jane died in 1751 and it seems likely that John then went to live with his uncle, Joshua Harle, a London grocer. Shortly after Jane's death, the contents of Rainham Hall were auctioned (the Hall itself was rented out). So, all the things that John Harle senior had collected during his life were dispersed; the house he built and fragments of written evidence are now our only window on his world.

Discovering John Harle's will

Some time ago, when at a car boot sale, a Rainham resident made an extraordinary connection with a dealer who sourced an original copy of John Harle's will. She generously donated it to Rainham Hall in 2014.

After John

Ownership of Rainham Hall passed out of the Harle family when John Harle junior died young. It was subsequently inhabited by a series of very different people.

John Harle and the Dearsleys

In 1758, the last remaining trustee of John Harle's 1742 will resigned. William Dearsley, a Hornchurch carpenter, was appointed sole trustee of orphaned, 18-year-old John junior. It may be that Dearsley rented Rainham Hall and the wharf after Jane Vincent's death in 1751.

In 1763, John Harle junior married William's daughter, Sarah. We know very little else about John Harle junior, but it seems his finances were in a bit of pickle. His father's estate had been left 'unadministered' and his mother, Sarah, had 'intermeddled' with it.

Like his father before him, John was an officer of Rainham parish council, but disappears from their records in 1766. It's around this time that John and Sarah became involved with the growing Methodist movement. Methodism was controversial with some Church of England followers, who regarded its practices as non-conformist – it's certainly clear that it was something with which Sarah's father did not agree (see 'Methodists and a mob' box).

Methodists and a mob

Followers of so-called 'non-conformist' religions like Methodism faced a number of issues in the 18th century: for instance they would be unlikely to get into university or obtain government or official posts. Even gathering to hear a preacher was not always safe.

On 12 March 1767, early Methodists assembled at Rainham Hall to hear a famous preacher. Among them was John Valton of Purfleet, a preacher himself and new friend of John and Sarah. But Sarah's father objected to the meeting. He threatened to horsewhip the preacher, who ran away upstairs, and he held Valton over the fire in the kitchen. Feeling Sarah's father had gone a bit too far, onlookers 'rescued' Valton, but turned him out to a mob gathered in the yard. The mob tore Valton's shirt, pulled his hair and suggested dunking him in the pond. He was glad to get back to Purfleet in one piece.

After John

John Harle junior died in 1770, aged 29. He was buried in his parents' grave at Rainham Church, perhaps reconciled to the Church of England. It seems that after John's death Sarah sold Rainham Hall to her father; he lived in the house, but returned it to her in his will.

In 1772, Sarah remarried to Jarvis Chambers, a successful haberdasher in the City of London. They lived in Hackney where two daughters were born, Susannah and Alicia Dearsley Chambers.

Ownership of Rainham Hall and the wharf passed down through the Chambers sisters and, in 1858, was left to the Reverend George Moreton Platt, a Yorkshire vicar who was a distant relative of their father. Neither the Chambers sisters nor the Reverend Platt lived at the Hall.

Far left and middle
Detail of the *trompe l'oeil* painting on the staircase that we believe was installed during Sarah Chambers' time at Rainham

Above and right
Sarah Chambers, nee Dearsley and Harle (above) and Jarvis Chambers (right), painted by renowned portrait artist, John Russell

The Daldy family

Rainham Hall and the wharf were again rented out, certainly from 1807, but perhaps earlier. For a short time it was a boarding school for 'young gentlemen', but from about 1809 Samuel Rootsey Daldy ran his coal business from the wharf and lived in the Hall. It must have been a lively time as Samuel and his wife Catherine had 12 children.

Catherine Daldy was widowed in 1834, but she carried on the coal business with the help of her second son Edward. Eventually Edward's youngest brother, Octavius George, joined him in the business and their mother retired to Bow, (then part of Middlesex). The Daldy brothers rented the property from the Reverend George Platt until they bought it from him in 1887. Although they continued their coal and timber trade from the wharf after 1860, they sub-let the Hall to various short-term tenants until 1874 when the Reverend Nicholas Brady moved in.

The Reverend Nicholas Brady

From 1874, the Daldys' subtenant (and, from 1887, their tenant) was the Reverend Nicholas Brady, rector of Wennington (Wennington parish didn't have a rectory), cycling enthusiast and amateur naturalist. Brady brought a period of stability in the tenanting of Rainham Hall.

The Reverend Brady was the son of Sir Anthony Brady, an official of the Navy Board who was also involved in the preservation of Epping Forest, in various seamen's missions, and in the East London Museum (now the Museum of Childhood, Bethnal Green). Both men were amateur naturalists of some note – Sir Anthony's collection of approximately 210,000-year-old bones from the Essex area is now in London's Natural History Museum. They were also very active in the Essex Naturalists' Field Club. Many of the members were apparently cycling enthusiasts, pedalling great distances to collect interesting specimens. Sir Anthony was an early member and president (from 1878–80) of the Pickwick Bicycle Club, the world's oldest cycling club, which was founded in Hackney in 1870.

Above Nicholas Brady with his cycling machine

A social beacon

Brady appears to have been quite hands-on at his Wennington parish; he introduced public baptisms, choral celebrations and evening services, and, partly due to his influence, a new school became a focus for the area's social life, hosting events from concerts to magic lantern shows to glee club meetings. In the 1880s, Brady also restored the church, which had become quite shabby by the time he moved in, and expanded it to accommodate Wennington's growing population.

Authors and astronomers: Brady's successful relations

Nicholas Brady's mother was related to the prolific children's authors Dorothy and Mary Ann Kilner who wrote stories such as *The Life and Perambulations of a Mouse* (1784) and *Little Stories for Little Folks* (1785). Reprinted into the 1870s, these are early examples of books written specifically for children.

On his father's side, Brady was related to Henry Perigal, a well-known astronomer and mathematician who proved Pythagoras' Theorem. His collection of scientific instruments are now in the Science Museum, London. When Perigal died in 1898, Nicholas Brady scattered his ashes at Wennington Church and erected a monument to him.

Brady at Rainham

In 1900, Nicholas Brady bought Rainham Hall. By this time the property consisted of just the house and gardens. The wharf, a field to the east of the gardens and small parcels of land along Wennington Road had been sold separately some time earlier.

Brady died in 1911, and is buried at Wennington. He left Rainham Hall to his wife Emma. They had no children, so in 1915 the Hall passed to Nicholas Brady's nieces and nephews.

Above Nicholas Brady in 1899; this image was presented to Wennington Church on the 25th anniversary of Brady's institution as rector

The 20th-century Hall

In the 1900s, Rainham Hall would experience a number of guises, from nursery to family home. But by the 1920s it was in a state of decay and so first it had to be restored.

Colonel Mulliner

Rainham's next owner after Brady was Colonel Herbert Hall Mulliner, an upmarket interior decorator, historian, fine art specialist and controversial restoration enthusiast. He came to Rainham looking for a new project.

Colonel (his title was an honorary one) Mulliner purchased Rainham Hall in 1917. Although his family background was in coach and automobile manufacturing, Mulliner turned to fine arts, becoming a director of decorating firm Lenyon & Co. He specialised in 18th-century furniture and was an antique collector of some note. His 1923 book *The Decorative Arts in England 1660–1780* is now classified as rare and expensive and some items from his collection are in the Victoria and Albert Museum, London.

Writing (and re-writing) history

In June 1920, Mulliner wrote about Rainham Hall for *Country Life* magazine. He didn't give any sources for his information, but all subsequent histories of the Hall were based on this article – until now. Thanks to our historical research team we know much more of the Hall's history than we did before.

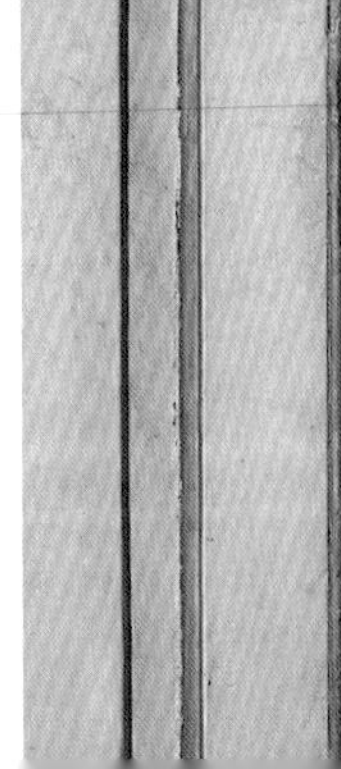

Right (above and below) Details of fittings we believe Mulliner installed at Rainham

A controversial figure

In 1912, Mulliner restored an 18th-century house in Soho, London, hoping to make a substantial profit on its sale. When he couldn't find a buyer he wanted to demolish the house. After public outcry, the property became subject to the first ever Preservation Order under the 1913 Ancient Monuments Act. But Mulliner appealed to the House of Lords and won his case, allowing him to sell the property for demolition. By 1919, the interior fittings such as fireplaces, room panelling, wall paintings and the oak staircase were stripped out by a salvage company and shipped to America (a not-uncommon practice with British heirlooms at the time). Here they were bought by millionaire Richard T. Crane junior for his new mansion in Massachusetts. Later the Crane family donated these interiors to the Art Institute of Chicago where they are now on display.

Mulliner's Rainham

Rainham Hall was Mulliner's next restoration project. His role as an architectural salvager is reflected in the things he added to the Hall, such as the railings and gates at the stable block and perhaps some fireplace fittings. These are from John Harle's era, but not original to the house.

The lack of 19th-century fittings and fixtures may be because Mulliner wanted to recreate his idea of an early 18th-century interior. However, he modernised the house by turning some of the bedrooms into bathrooms, moving the kitchen into the cellar, making the original kitchen into a study and modifying the stable block to take motor cars.

The coat of arms over the fireplace in the entrance hall is also a Mulliner addition. It was copied from the Harle grave in Rainham Church.

Mulliner never actually lived at Rainham Hall. His main home was in Rugby, and he had a flat in West London when he died in 1924.

Rainham's last owner: William Sturges

Following Mulliner's death, Rainham Hall was bought by (Francis) William Murray Sturges, Mulliner's solicitor and an executor of his estate.

William Sturges, his wife Nina and their six children lived at Rainham until the Second World War, when the Hall was requisitioned by Essex County Council as a nursery school and food distribution centre (see pages 14–15).

A new roof with attic rooms, dormer windows and attic staircase are the most obvious alterations Sturges made to the Hall. He also returned Mulliner's bathrooms to bedrooms.

Above Colonel Mulliner in conversation with Sir P A Munty, MP, in November 1907. Mulliner is on his horse

A wartime nursery

As with much of the country, the Second World War brought change and disruption to Rainham Hall when, in 1942, it was requisitioned by Essex County Council to be used as a nursery.

During the War, with the men away fighting, there was a shortage in Britain's workforce. In December 1941 conscription for women was brought in for the first time. Those conscripted, aged 19–50, could choose to go into the armed forces in non-combat roles, or to work on the land or in industry. Many Rainham women opted to work in the local factories contributing to the war effort. To allow mothers with young children to go out to work, the government, via local authorities, set up wartime nurseries. Many of these nurseries were housed in prefabricated buildings but the children of Rainham were lucky – they had the run of Rainham Hall and its gardens.

Appointed in January 1943, the first matron of Rainham day nursery was 40-year-old Miss Rhoda Violet Carter, who was assisted by two trained assistants and other staff. Her salary was £200 a year (the equivalent of about £10,000 today).

After the War, there was much debate in Parliament about what should happen to wartime nurseries, the benefits to families and whether this first government venture into childcare for under-fives should be continued. Many nurseries were closed but Rainham Hall stayed open until 1954.

'There cannot be many buildings of such historical value that can boast of having hundreds of tiny feet trotting through their grand hall! We had wonderful parties there at Christmas, Hallowe'en and Easter.

I can recall helping 30 or 40 two to five-year-olds climb two or three flights of stairs several times a day, washing in the underground washroom in a big wooden sink. And of course the secret door at the foot of the stairs, which was used as a nurses' coat room.'

Nurse Dorothy, a nursery nurse at Rainham Hall in the 1950s, quoted in the *Echo* newspaper

Right A poster encouraging women to help the war effort by working in factories

Not just a Nursery
Once a coach house and laundry, an outbuilding at Rainham Hall served as a Ministry of Food depot and first aid point during the War.

Above and left These images of the nursery were kindly shared with us by local resident Mrs Esme Hickin, a former nursery nurse at Rainham. The photos probably date from 1945–51

The National Trust comes to Rainham

Rainham Hall did not come to the Trust easily – there were two years where nobody knew what might happen to it at all.

When Sturges died in 1945, Rainham Hall was offered to the National Trust in lieu of paying death duties on the estate. This led to a period (from 1947–49) of uncertainty for the Hall. Consultations took place to decide which organisation might be able to make use of and care for the building. Surveyors felt it worthy of preservation but on the other hand, that its cause was not helped by the surrounding industrial development. The National Trust recognised its architectural significance but was reluctant to take it on without any source of income for its maintenance. As attempts to find a tenant failed, the Treasury wanted to reject the Hall as payment of death duties on Sturges's estate.

Eventually the Society for the Protection of Ancient Buildings (SPAB) – an organisation set up by William Morris that works to save old buildings from decay, demolition and damage – suggested that several of its supporters would be willing to take up the tenancy if the National Trust would take over the ownership. So in 1949, Rainham Hall was handed over to the National Trust.

The Trust's first tenants

As it turned out, Essex County Council had a firm tenancy agreement until 1954, so the Hall remained as a day nursery for a while longer.

When the day nursery moved out, Rainham Hall became a home again. It was leased to architectural historian Walter Ison and his wife, artist Leonora Payne. They were particularly interested in the Georgian architecture of Bath, where they had renovated a house. Walter wrote several architectural books, which Leonora illustrated. Public access to the Hall was limited, but the Isons gave tours on Wednesday and Saturday afternoons. Walter and Leonora stayed at Rainham Hall until 1962.

Left The gates and Corinthian porch from which Walter Ison got so much joy

'Stepping out each morning from underneath [Rainham's] fine Corinthian porch put a spring in Ison's step'

Christopher Woodward in Walter Ison's obituary, *The Independent*, 1997

Anthony Denney

In the 1960s, Rainham Hall became the home of Anthony Denney, an eccentric and well-known socialite photographer with an eye for modern art.

Denney (1913–1990) trained at the Royal College of Art, but it wasn't until after the Second World War that his artistic career really took off.

During the War, Denney served in the Royal Engineers, ultimately becoming a Captain in India and engaged in Military Intelligence. It was at this time that his work caught the eye of then-editor of British *Vogue*, Audrey Withers, and from 1947 Denney embarked on a career at *Vogue*'s parent company, Condé Nast. He remained there for over twenty years, his work appearing in *Vogue* and *House and Garden* magazines. He also became *Vogue*'s Decoration Editor, making him hugely influential on interior design at that time. Other projects included designing the interior of the Onassis family yacht and the 'G Plan gallery' in Hanover Square, London, a showroom for the G Plan company's pioneering furniture ranges.

Despite his association with the very of-the-time G Plan gallery, Denney collected 18th-century furniture, some of which he displayed at Rainham Hall. But he also had a talent for spotting up-and-coming modern artists before they were famous; he purchased works by Burri, Dubuffet, Fontana, Appel and Imai and built up an impressive modern art collection.

Above left Anthony Denney photographed by Christo Coetzee in the late 1950s or early 1960s

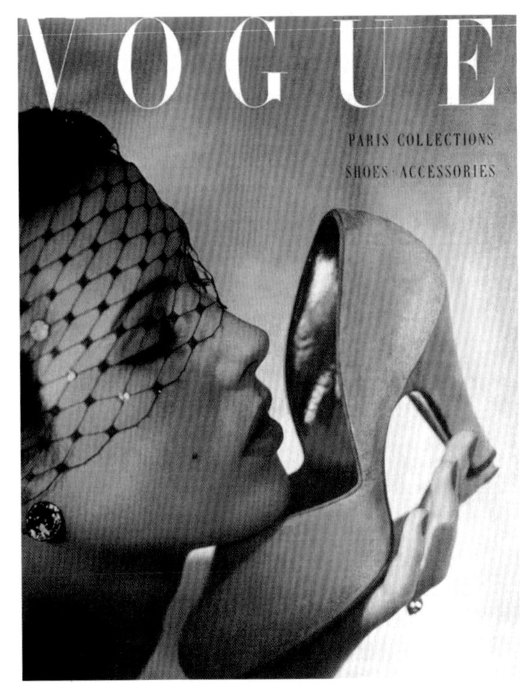

Right Denney's cover for the October 1950 edition of British *Vogue*

'To take refuge inside Rainham Hall is to step into another era, where beauty was cherished with every stroke of a painter's brush and with each deft move of a craftsman's chisel'

Hornchurch and Upminster Echo describing the Hall in 1966, during Denney's time here

Relationships

Denney was a friend of the influential cookery writer Elizabeth David, who is now credited with introducing the post-war British public to Mediterranean foods such as olive oil, pasta and Parmesan cheese. As well as decorating her Pimlico cookery shop, Denney illustrated David's book covers and articles for *Vogue*, and together they are credited with changing the way recipes were presented in magazines at the time.

Denney had also been married to children's author Diana Ross (who wrote the Little Red Engine books) but they were divorced by the time he moved to Rainham.

Restoring Rainham

Denney's interest in interior design may be what led him to Rainham Hall in *c.*1964. Soon after moving in as a tenant of the National Trust, he hired specialist workers who, over a number of years, painstakingly restored almost every room to how they might have looked when John Harle built them in the 18th century. However, the decor was not contemporary to Harles' time, but to a style three decades earlier; Denney wanted to reflect Harle's apparent desire for a 'good old fashioned house'.

We can still see Denney's colour schemes in the gilding and marbled paintwork in the entrance hall and wood panelling made to look like expensive oak – a trick favoured by the 18th-century artists Denney aimed to emulate.

Denney also employed a butler to supervise the day-to-day running of his household and oversee its internal redecoration.

Despite the effort he put into the Hall's restoration, Denney didn't remain there very long – he left in 1969. He later moved to Spain where he married his second wife, Celia Royde-Smith, and, in the 1980s, renovated a medieval castle. It was in Spain that he passed away, unexpectedly, in 1990.

Left One of the six largest furniture manufacturers in the UK in the 1950s, G Plan was pioneering for its modern designs, and for keeping designs in stock for a number of years to allow people to collect them slowly. Their sofas are some of the most well-known designs from the era, remaining popular today

The last tenants

After Anthony Denney left Rainham Hall, it was rented by a succession of talented musicians and artists. The Hall remained open to the public on select days (similar to the first tenants' arrangements, these were Wednesday afternoons from April to October only, and on Saturdays by prior appointment).

In the 1970s, architect Adrian Sansom and his wife Marilyn, a well-known cellist, lived at the Hall. They were followed, in the 1980s, by world-class viola player, Paul Silverthorne and his wife Mary – Paul is now the principal violist of the London Symphony Orchestra and London Sinfonietta. The Silverthornes encouraged Rainham residents to use the gardens and hosted charity events. Mary was quite sure the Hall was haunted by the ghost of Colonel Mulliner (see pages 12–13) – though only during the daytime; she described him as 'an incredibly friendly chap.'

Rainham would not have been an easy undertaking for the Silverthornes: 12-hour days of housework were not uncommon, and the Hall couldn't be subjected to modern equipment such as blowtorches, so DIY tasks had to be undertaken with much more basic kit like wire wool and white spirit. The original 1730s railings, which you can still see today, were also restored during the couple's tenancy.

'People always enjoy the visit and are sometimes surprised by it. They say the house has a very homely feel to it'

Juliet Roman in the *Romford & Havering Post*, 1988

'We feel privileged to be living here. Though we have our work cut out, it is a wonderful feeling to be able to call it home ... The gardens are lovely and if people would like to have their lunch on the grass, they only have to knock and let me know that they are there'

Mary Silverthorne in the *Romford Recorder*, 1984

Leaving their mark

The laughter and cries of young children rang through the Hall in the late 1980s and 1990s as TV and film set designer, Stefan Roman, his wife Juliet, and their two-year-son, Samuel, moved in. With the help of volunteers, the pair opened up new rooms including the master bedroom on the second floor. They also had a part-time gardener and housekeeper to help them run the home.

The Romans were followed by portrait artist David Atack (b.1949) and his young family. By this time one of the bedrooms was known as The Blue Room – Anthony Denney had painted it pale blue, but it was redecorated by a later tenant in the darker shade we see today.

Left The Blue Room in its present-day dark blue, which we know was painted after Anthony Denney's time at Rainham

Above right David Atack's self-portrait

The Rainham Restoration Project

Rainham Hall was occupied by National Trust tenants until 2010. When the building fell empty once more, a new and exciting prospect started to emerge.

Rather than just being a private residence, could the Hall become a centre for village life? Working with London Borough of Havering and the Heritage Lottery Fund, the National Trust asked Rainham: 'What would you want from the Hall?'

Our consultation made it clear that the Hall could be a centre for Rainham activity and a great new resource for the village. By restoring the stable block, we could create a new café and function room, connected to our one-hectare (three-acre) garden. This area, outside our traditional National Trust 'pay barrier' and accessible to everyone, could be a venue for craft workshops, summer fêtes, yoga classes, outdoor school lessons or meetings of local associations. Our plan for the Hall itself was to evoke the lives of past tenants, exploring the cultural, economic and historic themes around them to create programmes of activity.

Right The stable block during renovation work in 2015

Above left Volunteers at the front of Rainham Hall with its scaffolding during renovation works

Above right The door showing the many layers of paint added here by tenants over the years

What work's been done?

In June 2013, we were successfully awarded a Heritage Lottery Fund grant to realise our ambitions for the Hall and building work started in February 2014. The stable block has been the centre of activity, undergoing a full restoration that has elevated it far beyond its previous 'building at risk' status. A new roof, floors, heating system and heavily renovated brickwork has made the stable block ready to become a hive of commercial and community activity.

The Hall has undergone considerable repairs to its brickwork and been upgraded for modern use, receiving new heating, electrical and alarm systems. Internally, rotten panelling and shutters have been repaired but our decisions about decor were less straightforward.

Layers of history

It is in the paint of Rainham Hall's walls that the many layers of the building's past are truly represented. From Harle's simple, flat colours lying under layers of modern paint, to Anthony Denney's gilding, to later attempts at recreating the fashion for 'rag-rolling', each resident has left a layer, redolent of their time and taste. The Rainham Hall Project Team felt it would be a mistake to sweep these layers away and impose a single 'taste' upon this eclectic mix of styles and so we've sought to conserve as much decor as possible.

A community hub

Rainham Hall is now open to everyone, every day (the Hall itself is open five days a week in the open season). Our future purpose is simple: to provide a great daily resource for the people of Rainham and explore innovative ways to discover past residents and their lives at Rainham Hall. This ambitious new approach to a previously private residence is possible thanks to the far-sighted support of the Heritage Lottery Fund, London Borough of Havering and the people of Rainham who have become part of our project.